GET STARTED

Kathleen

STAMP
COLLECTING

FOR CANADIAN KIDS

KIDS CAN PRESS LTD., TORONTO

For Marilyn, with appreciation and love

Many thanks to the staff at Canada Post, especially Donna Reid and Deby Garnich.
Thanks also to stamp dealers John H. Talman Ltd. and George S. Wegg Ltd.
Special thanks to Andrew Graham-Hussey
and Greg Ioannou for generously sharing stamps from their collections.

Patricia Buckley worked incredibly hard to find all the stamps in the book,
Bill Slavin and Esperança Melo beautifully illustrated everything else,
and Marie Bartholomew made everything look great together. As always, it was a
pleasure to be edited by Val Wyatt — what more can I say?! Thanks to all the staff at
Kids Can Press, especially Lori Burwash, Ricky Englander and Valerie Hussey.
Much love to Paul for all his support and help.

Kids Can Press Ltd. acknowledges with appreciation the assistance of the Canada Council and the Ontario Arts Council in the production of this book.

Canadian Cataloguing in Publication Data

MacLeod, Elizabeth
    Stamp collecting : for Canadian kids

At head of title: Get started.
ISBN 1-55074-279-5 (bound)
ISBN 1-55074-313-9 (pbk.)

1. Stamp collecting - Canada - Juvenile literature.
2. Stamp collecting - Juvenile literature. I. Slavin, Bill. II. Melo, Esperança. III. Title. IV. Title: Get started.

HE6213.M33   1996   j769.56'075   C95-933339-8

Text copyright © 1996 by Elizabeth MacLeod
Illustrations copyright © 1996 by Esperança Melo
   and Bill Slavin

All Canadian stamps reproduced courtesy of Canada Post Corporation.

The stamp catalogue page that appears on page 9 is from *Unitrade Specialized Catalogue of Canadian Stamps 1995*. Used with permission of Unitrade Associates.

Produced with assistance from the RPSC Philatelic Research Foundation, Ottawa.

Credits, pages 24–25:
St. Lawrence Seaway
 — *National Archives of Canada/POS-000439*
St. Lawrence Seaway (mistake)
 — *National Archives of Canada/POS-002662*

Prairie Street
 — *National Archives of Canada/POS-000776*
Prairie Street (mistake)
 — *National Archives of Canada/1993-045*

Kids Can Press Ltd.
29 Birch Avenue
Toronto, Ontario, Canada   M4V 1E2

Edited by Valerie Wyatt
Designed by Marie Bartholomew
Stamps researched by Patricia Buckley
Printed in Hong Kong by
  Wing King Tong Company Limited

96 0 9 8 7 6 5 4 3 2 1
PA 96 0 9 8 7 6 5 4 3 2 1

CONTENTS

Getting Started with Stamps	4
Stamp Parts	6
Stamp Stuff	8
Talk the Talk	10
Taking Care of Your Stamps	12
What to Collect?	14
Making a Stamp Album	16
It's in the Mail	18
Special Delivery	20
Birth of a Stamp	22
Oops! – Stamp Mistakes	24
Weird and Wonderful	26
Where in the World?	28
What to Look For	30
It's Incredible	32
Beyond Stamps	34
Keeping You Posted	36
Collecting Canadian Stamps	38
More Stamp Talk	39
Index	40

GETTING STARTED WITH STAMPS

Do you want to collect stamps? This book will show you how. Once you get started, you'll see why stamp collecting is the most popular hobby in the world. Become a stamp collector and you'll make new friends, explore Canada and travel the world without ever leaving home. Best of all, starting a stamp collection doesn't take up a lot of room or cost a lot of money.

Here are some of the most incredible stamps you'll ever find – in Canada *or* around the world.

The world's **first stamp** was issued in Great Britain on May 6, 1840. It's called the Penny Black.

The 1856 British Guiana one-cent stamp is the **rarest stamp**. There's only one left in the whole world, and it's worth more than $1 million.

The world's **smallest stamps** were issued in 1856 by the German state of Mecklenberg-Schwerin. The stamps were sold only in groups of four, but each one is just 9 mm × 9 mm ($\frac{3}{8}$ in. × $\frac{3}{8}$ in.) – so small that it would fit on the nail of your pointer finger.

Most experts agree that the world's **biggest stamp** was issued in China between 1905 and 1912. It was the same size as the one on the right. Only one part of it (the dragon's body) was actually used on letters.

Canada's first stamp was the Three-Penny Beaver, issued April 23, 1851. It was also the first stamp in the world with an animal on it. Sir Sandford Fleming designed it. He's the man who divided the world into time zones and who helped get the railroad built across Canada.

Before Canada's provinces joined to make one country, they issued their own stamps. The world's **first diamond-shaped stamp** was issued by Nova Scotia on September 1, 1851.

The world's **first Christmas stamp** was issued in Canada in 1898.

STAMP PARTS

Every stamp tells a story – you just have to know how to read it. You can find out where a stamp is from, how much it cost, why it was issued, and much more just by looking at it carefully.

Perforations, or **perfs**, are the holes between stamps. Some stamps have perfs on only two or three sides. Early stamps had no perfs and had to be cut apart. They are called imperforates.

The **borderline** is the edge of the picture.

The **margin** is the blank space between the picture and the perforations.

The **country** that issued the stamp.

The name of the **artist** who drew the picture sometimes appears on the stamp. Sometimes the **designer's** name also appears. The designer chooses the style of the lettering and puts it together with the picture.

Some designs include a **description** of why the stamp was issued.

CANADA

Rainbow trout · La truite arc-en

E. MELO / M. BARTH

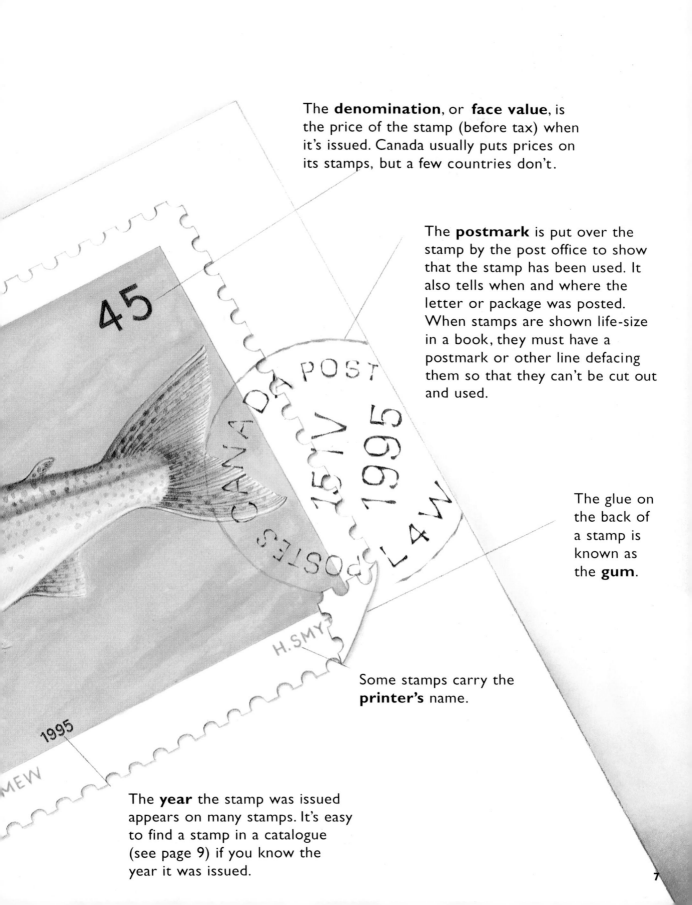

The **denomination**, or **face value**, is the price of the stamp (before tax) when it's issued. Canada usually puts prices on its stamps, but a few countries don't.

The **postmark** is put over the stamp by the post office to show that the stamp has been used. It also tells when and where the letter or package was posted. When stamps are shown life-size in a book, they must have a postmark or other line defacing them so that they can't be cut out and used.

The glue on the back of a stamp is known as the **gum**.

Some stamps carry the **printer's** name.

The **year** the stamp was issued appears on many stamps. It's easy to find a stamp in a catalogue (see page 9) if you know the year it was issued.

STAMP STUFF

Camping, soccer, stamp collecting – they're all easier and more fun if you have the right equipment. You can buy the stuff to start your stamp collection for less than $20.

Stamps

Ask friends and family to save stamps for you. To give your collection a kick-start, you might want to buy a bag of stamps from around the world. These bags cost about $5 for 500 stamps.

Stamps can also be bought at stamp clubs, auctions and shows or from dealers. Find out more about these sources on page 36.

Albums

Some albums have pictures of stamps printed right in them. When you find one of the stamps shown, you attach it on top of its picture. These albums sell for about $10. They're well organized but can be frustrating if you can't find all the stamps shown.

Other albums are blank. *You* choose which stamps to include and how to arrange them. (For tips, see page 16.) Blank album pages sell for about $6 for 50 pages and can be kept in a three-ring binder.

Remember – your stamp collection will grow. Choose an album that lets you add pages.

Tongs

Even clean hands leave fingerprints, dirt, oil and moisture. Oil can change a stamp's colour or damage the gum, and wetness makes a stamp curl. Handle valuable stamps with tongs or tweezers, which can be bought for about $4. Use round-ended tongs to avoid tearing stamps.

Hinges

Hinges are small pieces of transparent paper with gum on one side that are used to stick stamps in an album. You can also unstick them and remove the stamps later if you wish.

Plastic mounts

These are clear plastic strips with gummed backings. You stick the mount in your album, then slip in your stamp. You can buy plastic mounts in long strips or already cut for single stamps. Save them for special stamps since they're more expensive than hinges.

Catalogues and guides

Most countries publish catalogues of their stamps every year. You can see a page from one below. Catalogues help you find what stamps are available.

You can also buy colour guides to check the exact colour of your stamps and perforation guides to help you count the number of perfs. Collectors who sell or trade stamps use these guides to help them describe their stamps.

Magnifying glass

To examine a stamp for tears and other damage, you'll need a magnifier. A good basic magnifying glass costs about $2.

OCTOBER 1, 1993. PREHISTORIC LIFE IN CANADA – 3

Perf. 13½ Pane of 20 DINOSAURS

Qty.

1495	43¢ Massospondylus (Jurassic period)	
1496	43¢ Styracosaurus (Cretaceous period)	
1497	43¢ Albertosaurus (Cretaceous period)	
1498 a	43¢ Plateca...	17,000M

This ... se-to...

TALK THE TALK

Stamp collectors have their own language. For example, they call themselves philatelists *(fill-at-a-lists)*. Stamp collecting is philately *(fill-at-a-lee)*. Stamp collectors also have special names for stamps.

Definitives: Stamps that are printed many times, in large numbers and sold for many years. They usually feature symbols of the country they're from. On Canadian definitives you'll find Queen Elizabeth, the Houses of Parliament in Ottawa, Canada's flag, etc.

Pictorials:

Any stamp with a picture on it. Most stamps today are pictorials, but a few have designs instead of pictures. Some old stamps have no pictures, just words, numbers or symbols.

Commemoratives: Stamps issued to celebrate a special event or to honour a person, place or anniversary. Only a limited number are printed.

Semi-postals: Stamps that cost the price of postage *plus* a small extra amount. The extra money is donated to a charity or special fund.

Special issues: Stamps that show scenes or other things from the country that issues them. They're larger than definitives and, unlike commemoratives, aren't issued to commemorate something.

Used stamps: Stamps that have been postmarked. Used stamps may be worth as much as mint stamps if they're in good condition. Most collectors collect either mint stamps or used stamps. Not both.

Mint stamps: New or never-mailed stamps. All stamps are mint stamps when they are issued.

More stamp talk
Cinderellas and killers? Traffic light in the gutter? Huh? Turn to page 39 for a translation and more stamp terms.

TAKING CARE OF YOUR STAMPS

Most stamps come stuck to envelopes. Here's how to remove them and use hinges or mounts to put them in an album.

Peeling a stamp from an envelope

I. Fill a bowl with room-temperature water.

2. Cut the stamp off the envelope, leaving a bit of the envelope around it. Float the stamp picture-side up in the water.

3. Wait for 15 minutes, then try to peel a corner of the envelope away from the stamp. (Don't peel the stamp – you might tear it.) If you can't, put it back in the water for another 5 minutes.

TIP
• If you're removing stamps from different colours of envelopes, use one bowl of water for each colour. This keeps the dyes in the envelope paper from staining other stamps. Working quickly helps, too!

4. If a corner of the envelope will lift away from the stamp, it's ready. Place the stamp picture-side down on the palm of one hand and gently lift off the envelope. Use your fingers to remove stamps – tongs might damage the stamp.

5. Lay the stamp picture-side down on a clean paper towel and gently blot it dry with another paper towel.

6. Flatten the stamp by putting it between two paper towels and placing a book on top. Leave it overnight.

Sticking a stamp in an album

Once your stamps are dry, put them in an album to keep them safe. Use hinges for sticking less expensive stamps in your album and plastic mounts for more valuable stamps.

To use a hinge, slightly wet the short end of the hinge and attach it to the back of the stamp. The hinge should be stuck as near to the top as possible without showing from the front of the stamp. Wet the bottom part of the other end of the hinge and stick your stamp to the album page.

hinge

plastic mount

To use a plastic mount, wet the back of the plastic mount or remove the backing paper and stick the mount into your album. Slip the stamp into the mount as shown. Unlike a hinge, the mount isn't attached to the stamp, so it doesn't damage the stamp.

WHAT TO COLLECT?

When you start out, you'll probably collect every stamp you can find. But soon you may want to specialize in one kind of stamp. How do you pick a subject?

- Are you a Girl Guide or Boy Scout? Look for stamps about your group.

- If you draw or paint, collect stamps that highlight art.

- If you like to travel, collect stamps from the countries you want to visit.

- Find out about your own country by collecting Canada's stamps.

- Collect stamps from the year you were born.

The stamps on this page will give you other ideas. See page 34 for more stamp-related stuff to collect.

Sports
Such as hockey, Summer Olympic Games, baseball and football.

Animals
Including dogs of Canada, endangered animals and wildlife, and Canada's butterflies.

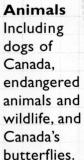

Famous Canadians

Including: Jeanne Sauvé, Canada's first female governor general; Terry Fox, who ran partway across Canada to raise money for cancer research; Chief Crowfoot, who prevented war between Canada and the Blackfoot in the 1870s; Josiah Henson, who operated an escape route into Canada for American slaves; Anne of Green Gables.

Prepacks

Packages of stamps like the one above contain Canadian stamps issued over several months.

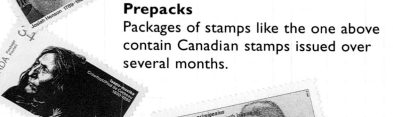

Space

Including the Canadarm, the launching of the *Alouette II* satellite, Canadians in space and satellite technology.

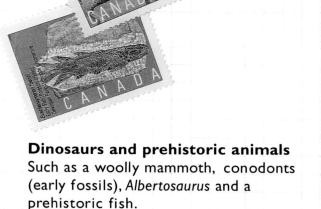

Dinosaurs and prehistoric animals

Such as a woolly mammoth, conodonts (early fossils), *Albertosaurus* and a prehistoric fish.

MAKING A STAMP ALBUM

Putting your stamps into an album can turn a pile of stamps into a real collection. If you are using a blank album, here's how to get started.

1. Divide the stamps into groups of similar stamps. For instance, if you collect animal stamps, put all the birds together, all the bears in another group, and so on.

2. Lay the stamps out on a right- or left-hand page of the album. (Don't put stamps on facing pages – they might become damaged.) Leave space at the top of the page for a title and room under each stamp for a label (more about that later). Keep some space blank for stamps you may collect in the future.

3. When you're happy with the layout, lightly mark where you want to place the stamps by putting dots at the corners.

4. Write labels for each stamp, like the one below. Use black ink – coloured inks will take attention away from the stamps. Or output the information on a computer, then cut out each description and paste it into your album.

The peregrine falcon is one of the fastest birds in the world.

5. Use hinges to stick the stamps in place. (See page 13 for how to use hinges.) Make a mistake? Let the hinge dry for at least ten minutes, then peel the hinge and stamp off the album page.

TIPS
• Draw a faint line down the middle of the page to help you centre the stamps. Erase the line before you attach the stamps.

• Try different layouts in the same album. Variety adds interest.

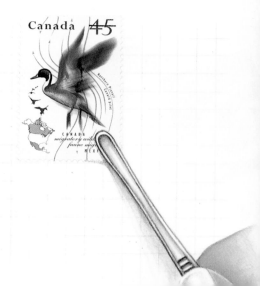

BIRD STAMPS

Issued for International Literacy Year, 1990. The bird stands for the freedom to read.

Drawn by an Inuit artist for the International Year of the World's Indigenous People, 1993.

The thunderbird is an Ojibwa symbol.

One of four stamps issued to celebrate Christmas 1973.

The great horned owl is Alberta's provincial bird.

The belted kingfisher migrates to Mexico every winter.

Definitive stamp of a decoy used between 1982 and 1987.

The peregrine falcon is one of the fastest birds in the world.

TIP
• If you see an interesting layout in a book or at a show, make a sketch so you'll remember it.

IT'S IN THE MAIL

Do you like sending – or better still, getting – letters in the mail? If so, you're not alone. As soon as human beings developed a written language, they wanted to exchange letters.

The first postal service began in China about 6000 years ago. There weren't any stamps – people simply paid a messenger to deliver their letters. From 550 to 333 B.C., horseback messengers travelled between important cities from the Mediterranean to India, delivering mail long-distance. A messenger would ride to a relay station, then pass the letter to another messenger and so on, until the letter reached its destination.

By the year 300, letters were carried through much of Europe by a postal system based in Rome, Italy. Sometimes messengers travelled by horse, sometimes on foot. By the 1400s there were many postal services in Europe, run

by royalty, business people, universities, monasteries and large towns and cities. A hundred years later, most of these postal services were owned by royalty. Some were still in operation as late as the 1860s.

In North America, postal systems were also developing. The first regular mail route in Canada began in 1763. Men on horseback delivered mail between Quebec City, Trois-Rivières and Montreal.

Back on the other side of the ocean, the British postal system was in trouble. People had found ways to send mail free. If you sent a letter to a friend in Britain, you didn't have to pay for postage – your

friend did. To avoid the costs, the sender sometimes put a coded message on the envelope. The receiver got the message just by looking at the envelope – without having to pay a cent. There were other problems, too. Many people refused to spend money for letters they didn't want, so the post office ended up carrying a lot of letters for nothing.

In 1837 Sir Rowland Hill was given the job of fixing the system. He came up with the idea that the person *mailing* the letter had to pay for it. What was needed was a way to show that the letter had been paid for. That's why stamps were invented. They told the post office that a certain amount of money had been paid to send the letter. The world's first postage stamp was the Penny Black, issued in 1840. Finally, there was an easy, inexpensive postal system that everyone could use.

In less than 40 years, Sir Rowland's stamp system spread to more than 150 countries. Suddenly people everywhere had a new hobby – stamp collecting!

Sir Rowland Hill

What's in the mail?

Paper was invented in China about 200 B.C. Lightweight and cheap, it's still our choice for letter writing more than 2000 years later. It took a while for paper to spread around the world. In the meantime, there were some pretty strange things in the mail. For example, long ago people in Asia wrote letters on clay tablets and baked them until hard. Even the envelopes were clay. Later, the Egyptians, Greeks and Romans wrote on papyrus made by pounding stems of the papyrus plant together. Since papyrus was too stiff to fold, letters were often rolled instead. Animal skins were tanned to make a writing surface called parchment. Poorly tanned skins sometimes curled back into the shape of the animal they had come from.

What does the future hold for letter writers? Some people claim that E-mail (electronic mail) will replace paper letters. That raises an important question for philatelists: Will there be E-stamps?

SPECIAL DELIVERY

Stick a stamp on a letter and pop it into a mailbox. Your letter has started on a journey that may take it across the country or around the world by truck, boat or plane. Or maybe by reindeer, camels or even cats?

In 1879 a letter in the city of Liege, Belgium, might have been delivered by a cat. This "puss post" didn't last long – as every cat owner knows, cats aren't very good at following orders.

You might say this mail was in the bag. In the early 1900s, people on the remote Scottish island of St. Kilda put letters into a waterproof bag made from part of a sheep's stomach and tossed it into the sea. When the bag drifted to the mainland, the person who found it would mail the letters inside.

Letters have also travelled by reindeer, camel and llama. Horses were important mail carriers – the famous Pony Express moved mail across the western United States in the 1800s. Even pigeons have been used to carry the mail – in the Netherlands as early as 1575. No heavy parcels, please!

The only underwater post office in the world is located in the Bahamas. It's in a glass-walled globe on the sea floor. The postmark on letters mailed there is: SEA FLOOR / BAHAMAS.

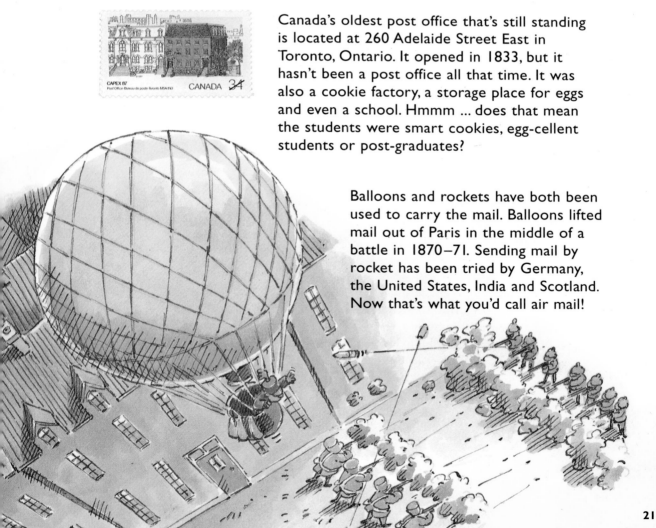

Canada's oldest post office that's still standing is located at 260 Adelaide Street East in Toronto, Ontario. It opened in 1833, but it hasn't been a post office all that time. It was also a cookie factory, a storage place for eggs and even a school. Hmmm ... does that mean the students were smart cookies, egg-cellent students or post-graduates?

Balloons and rockets have both been used to carry the mail. Balloons lifted mail out of Paris in the middle of a battle in 1870–71. Sending mail by rocket has been tried by Germany, the United States, India and Scotland. Now that's what you'd call air mail!

BIRTH OF A STAMP

It takes about two years to design and print a new stamp. Here's the story of one stamp, from idea to lick and stick.

The idea

Every year hundreds of Canadians write to Canada Post Corporation (CPC) to suggest new stamp ideas. CPC also comes up with its own ideas. To choose the best, all the ideas go to CPC's Stamp Advisory Committee, which is made up of 12 stamp collectors, historians, designers and business people. It is their job to choose 12 to 15 subjects for each year's stamps.

Research

Once a subject gets the committee's stamp of approval, a research team gathers information about it. That material is handed over to a design manager who checks books and talks to experts to find out what should be shown on each stamp and what mistakes to avoid. He also gathers the best pictures and references for each stamp's image. This can take several months.

The design

The design manager asks a number of artists to submit their ideas for the stamp. These trial designs are known as design proposals. They include the artwork as well as the denomination and other wording needed on the stamp. The designs are submitted to the Stamp Advisory Committee, which considers them carefully. Even when the final design is chosen, the artist may be asked to make slight changes to it.

To illustrate a Bombardier Ski-doo stamp, the artist works from a photograph.

The artwork

It takes about a month for the artist to create the artwork for one stamp. The art is often four or five times larger than the actual stamp will be. Why? Creating a detailed piece of art the size of a stamp would be difficult. When the art is complete, the lettering is added, and the stamp is sent to the printer.

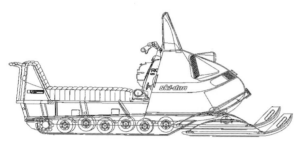

Using a computer, the artist produces a drawing of the Bombardier Ski-doo.

The artist uses the computer to fill in the colour.

The printing

The printer first makes a sample, called a proof, so that CPC can check it and make sure that the final stamp will look just the way it should. Many proofs and corrections may be needed to make sure the stamp is perfect.

Once the proof is approved, the stamp is printed on large sheets of paper called press sheets. Stamp printing presses can print as many as three million stamps an hour. The press sheets are then cut into smaller sheets called panes and perforated. The perfs are made by passing the panes through a machine called a perforator, which pierces the sheet with a row of needles that looks like a comb. Then the stamps are inspected one last time to make sure there are no flaws.

Delivering the stamp

Every new stamp has a day of issue that is set by CPC. You might say it's the stamp's birth date. About two weeks ahead of this birth date, the stamps are shipped to postal outlets across Canada so that they're ready for the day of issue. And ready for you to stick on an envelope – or add to your collection!

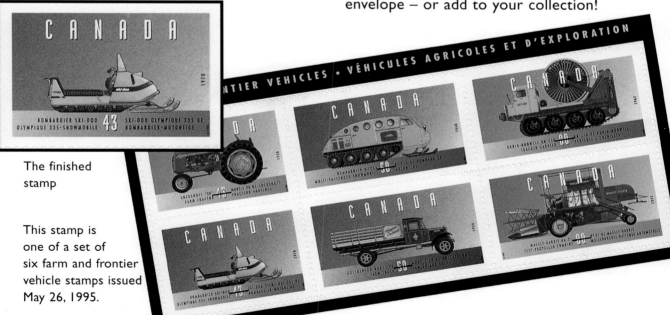

The finished stamp

This stamp is one of a set of six farm and frontier vehicle stamps issued May 26, 1995.

OOPS! – STAMP MISTAKES

If you find a stamp with an error, treat it with care. Why? It's rare and therefore more valuable than a perfect stamp. Usually printing errors are found before the stamps go on sale, and the stamps are destroyed. Sometimes stamps with an error are deliberately printed in huge numbers so that they are no longer rare and valuable. Here are some of the most famous and expensive Canadian stamp mistakes, as well as some cheaper ones you may want to add to your collection.

Probably the most famous Canadian stamp error is the St. Lawrence Seaway stamp. It was issued on June 26, 1959, to mark the opening of the seaway. Hundreds of stamps had the picture upside down – this is known as an **inverted centre**. When the stamps were issued, they cost 5¢. Today, each is worth about $14 500.

A **constant variety** is an error that appears in the same position on each sheet of an entire printing of a stamp. This Hudson Bay Discovered stamp, issued as part of a block of four on August 29, 1986, has an error that's earned it the name "Pink Panther." Why? It has a pink patch that doesn't appear on the regular stamp. You can buy this Pink Panther block of stamps for about $5. Can you tell if the stamps at the top of this page are regular stamps or Pink Panthers?

An **inconstant variety** is a mistake that is always in the same place but does not appear on all sheets of the stamps. This stamp of polar bears was released September 8, 1972. Look closely at the space between the polar bears on the regular version above and on the stamp with the error on the left. This "Siamese bears" variety is worth about $35.

If a mistake is made during the perforating of stamps, the stamps may end up with a **perfing error**, such as no perforations, partial perfs or perfs through the picture. You can see this third type of error on the definitive shown here. Today it's worth about $25.

Paper folds happen when stamps are printed on paper that's folded or creased. This Queen Elizabeth definitive with a paper fold was issued February 8, 1967, and is now worth about $15.

Oddities and **freaks** are extreme flaws that usually end up being thrown out. However, some are accidentally issued. An example is this Prairie Street stamp, issued in 1978. It's known as the "ghost town" variety because the scene looks empty. It has increased in value from 50¢ to about $3000.

A **printing shift** occurs when the perfs are in the right place but the picture isn't. Without an error, this definitive, issued in 1977, is now worth about 6¢. With the printing shift it costs $50.

WEIRD AND WONDERFUL

Stamps are four-sided pieces of paper, right? Not always. Take a look at these oddballs and collectibles.

Some countries issue stamps that are shaped like the countries themselves. This stamp is from Sierra Leone. It was also the first stamp you didn't have to lick — it has a self-adhesive backing. The stamp is part of a set of seven that sells for $7.

This is Canada's first hologram stamp. It was issued on October 1, 1992, to honour Canadian achievements in space. The map of Canada appears and disappears as you tilt the stamp. In mint condition, one of these stamps would cost just over $1.

Canada issued the world's first "do-it-yourself" stamps on January 28, 1994. You could add stickers to personalize the stamps for birthdays or other special occasions. You could even draw pictures on them. A top-quality do-it-your-selfer sells for less than $1.

Here's a stamp shape you don't see very often — a triangle. These stamps from the African country of Chad cost less than $2 for the pair. If you have stamps like these in your collection, keep them joined.

Canada ~~30~~

Canada ~~60~~

Canada ~~35~~

Dream of owning a Three-Penny Beaver? Although a high-quality original (see page 5) is now worth $20 000, this reissue (top) costs less than $1. An original *Bluenose* stamp, issued January 8, 1929, is worth $300 in top quality, but you can buy this reissue (middle) for less than $2. The RCMP stamp (bottom) was the first issued in Canada with a date hidden in the design. Can you find it?

Tonga, a country made up of more than 150 islands in the Pacific Ocean, is famous for its unusual stamps. This heart-shaped stamp, issued in 1964, not only has an unusual shape, it's also printed on foil, not paper.

Mmmm! These a-PEEL-ing stamps were issued by Tonga in 1969. Tonga has issued more than 600 self-adhesive stamps, some shaped like watches, parrots, even bananas!

This stamp-map of one of the Tonga islands, issued in 1964, was printed on silver foil. Despite the silver, the price is a reasonable $5 for a set of six stamps.

The South Asian country of Bhutan issued these three-dimensional stamps that sell for about $1 each. The birds pop out of the background and you can almost feel the feathers.

WHERE IN THE WORLD?

Did you know that a stamp with the name Hellas on it is from Greece? Sometimes it's hard to tell which country a stamp comes from because the name on the stamp isn't in English. Here's a list of countries and their names as they appear on their stamps. Use this list to identify your stamps, as well as the stamps on these pages. (Got a stamp with a name that isn't listed here? A stamp dealer can help you identify it.)

Name that appears on stamp	Country
België or Belgique	Belgium
Brasil	Brazil
Cambodge	Cambodia
CCCP	the former Soviet Union
Côte d'Ivoire	Ivory Coast
Danmark	Denmark
Deutsche Bundespost	Germany (West)
DDR	Germany (East)
Eesti	Estonia
Eire	Ireland (Republic)
España or Española	Spain
Hellas	Greece
Helvetia	Switzerland
Island	Iceland
Jugoslavija	Yugoslavia
Kibris	Cyprus
KSA	Saudi Arabia
LAR	Libya
Liban or Libanaise	Lebanon
Lietuva	Lithuania
Magyar or Magyarorszag	Hungary
Maroc	Morocco
Moçambique	Mozambique
Nippon	Japan
Norge	Norway
Persanes	Iran
Pilipinas	Philippines
Polska	Poland
Pulau Pinang	Penang
République Dominicana	Dominican Republic
République Française	France
Republik Österreich	Austria
RSA	South Africa
Salvador	El Salvador
Siam	Thailand
Suomi	Finland
Sverige	Sweden
Tchad	Chad
Toga	Tonga
Tunisie or Tunisienne	Tunisia
UAE	United Arab Emirates
UAR	Egypt or Syria
Viet-nam Cong-Hoa	South Vietnam
Viet-nam Dan Chu Cong Hoa	North Vietnam

WHAT TO LOOK FOR

Even experts sometimes disagree on what makes one stamp better than another, but here are some things to look for when buying stamps.

MINT STAMPS

Very fine
Like all mint stamps, very fine mint stamps have never been used. The margins are even, the colours bright, and there are no tears. The gum is undamaged or has not had a hinge attached.

Fine
The margins aren't even, but the perfs don't touch the design. It isn't faded, but it's not as bright as a very fine. The paper has small flaws but no tears or creases. The gum is slightly damaged.

Very good
The margins can be quite uneven – the perfs may touch the design. These stamps are slightly faded with tears, creases or stains. The gum is damaged or missing in places.

USED STAMPS

Very fine
These used stamps are bright and the paper is undamaged. The design has even margins, and the postmark is light, clear and centred. The gum is complete or shows that the stamp has had a hinge.

Fine
The colour isn't as bright as very fine stamps. The paper has small flaws but no tears or creases. The margins are uneven and the gum is disturbed slightly. The postmark is clear.

Very good
The colour is faded, and the paper may be creased or stained. The perfs may touch the design, and the postmark may not be readable. The gum is disturbed or partially missing.

GROUPS OF STAMPS

Some people don't collect just single stamps; they collect groups of stamps. Here are some groups to look for.

▲ **Twins:** A pair of stamps that form one large picture when joined or two small pictures when separated. If you have twins in your collection, leave them joined.

▼ **Strip:** Three or more stamps joined in a horizontal or vertical row.

▼ **Block:** Four or more stamps joined together in a square or rectangle. A corner block is shown here.

▲ **Se-tenant** (French for "joined together"): Two or more stamps that are joined together and that have different values or designs.

▲ **Coil:** A long roll of stamps that often have perfs on only two sides.

IT'S INCREDIBLE

Stamps have been used to decorate walls and build canals – they have even started wars! Read on to discover some incredible stamp stories.

When Great Britain issued the world's first stamp, the Penny Black (see page 4), in 1840, people wallpapered rooms and decorated fans and vases with it. The stamp was originally worth 1¢, but now it's worth more than $7000 in top condition.

No one in the world has been on more stamps than Queen Elizabeth II. Since becoming queen on February 6, 1952, she has appeared on about 10 000 stamps.

The youngest person ever to design a stamp was Samantha Brown, who was five when she painted a 1981 Christmas stamp for Great Britain.

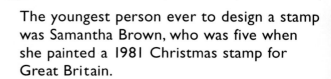

In 1930, Bolivia issued a stamp showing a map of the country. The stamp-map included an area that the neighbouring country of Paraguay said belonged to it. The stamp started a war that lasted until 1939, when the disputed land was finally given to Paraguay.

When a canal was being planned to link the Atlantic and Pacific oceans in Central America in the early 1900s, no one could decide whether it should be built in Panama or Nicaragua. By chance, Nicaragua had just issued two stamps showing its volcanic mountain, Mount Momotombo. Even though the mountain had been dormant for years, the stamps showed the volcano erupting. They made Nicaragua look dangerous, and the canal was built in Panama instead. You might say the Panama Canal owes its existence to stamps.

The world's rarest and most valuable stamp, the 1856 British Guiana one cent (see page 4), was found by a 12-year-old named Vernon Vaughan in 1873. He stumbled across it while looking through some old letters he'd found in the attic of his home in British Guiana. The stamp was drab and in poor condition, and Vaughan needed money to buy more colourful stamps. So he traded it for less than a dollar. Now the stamp is worth more than $1 million.

Because Great Britain issued the first stamp in the world, it has the special honour of not having to put its name on its stamps. It's the only country allowed to do this. Some countries, such as the United States, use just their initials. Others, such as Saudi Arabia, use a symbol of their country with their initials.

Like all stamps from Great Britain, this stamp doesn't include the country's name. But it does include a silhouette of Queen Elizabeth. Can you find it?

BEYOND STAMPS

Jour d'émission
Société canadienne des postes

Stamp collectors sometimes collect other postal stuff, too.

Official first-day covers ▶ are specially designed envelopes sold to go with new stamps. The postmark on a first-day cover is the same date as the issue day of the stamps. Canada began issuing first-day covers in 1971.

▼ Stamps issued in groups of eight or more in a thin cardboard wrapper are known as **booklets.** Usually the wrapper contains information about the stamps.

▲ **Postmarks** are the markings printed over a stamp by the post office. Collectors like them because they tell stories about letters by showing when and where they were posted.

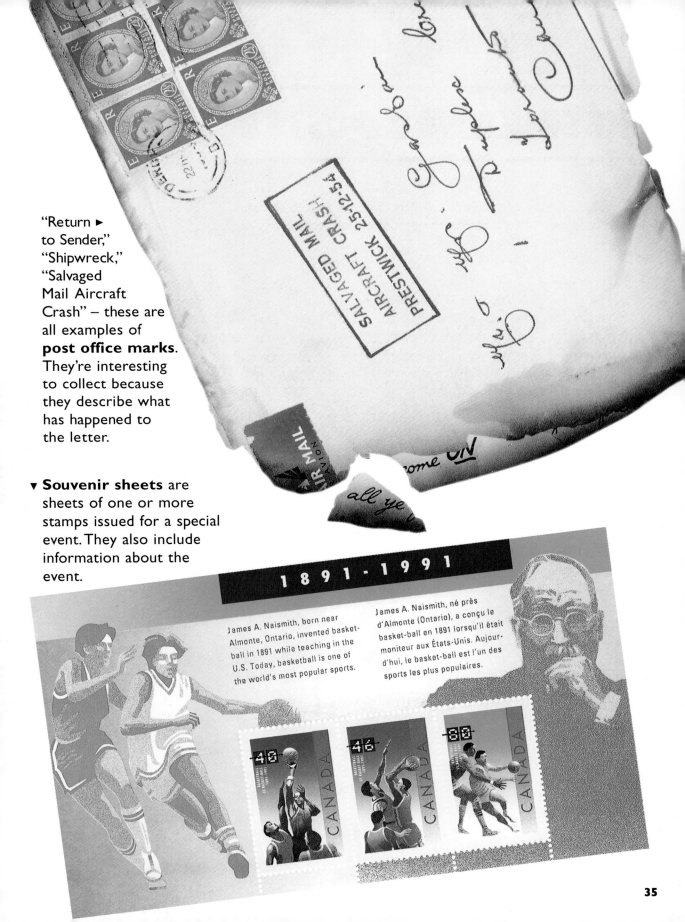

"Return ▶ to Sender," "Shipwreck," "Salvaged Mail Aircraft Crash" – these are all examples of **post office marks**. They're interesting to collect because they describe what has happened to the letter.

SALVAGED MAIL
AIRCRAFT CRASH 25·12·54
PRESTWICK

▼ **Souvenir sheets** are sheets of one or more stamps issued for a special event. They also include information about the event.

1891 - 1991

James A. Naismith, born near Almonte, Ontario, invented basketball in 1891 while teaching in the U.S. Today, basketball is one of the world's most popular sports.

James A. Naismith, né près d'Almonte (Ontario), a conçu le basket-ball en 1891 lorsqu'il était moniteur aux États-Unis. Aujourd'hui, le basket-ball est l'un des sports les plus populaires.

KEEPING YOU POSTED

There are lots of ways to find out more about stamps, add to your collection or meet other collectors.

Stamp clubs

Join a stamp club and you'll meet other collectors, maybe even make a foreign pen-pal. You'll also take part in displays, contests and stamp swaps. And you'll learn more about stamps and other stamp stuff by attending talks by experts or going on excursions.

To find a club to join, check your school – many schools have stamp clubs. If your parents or anyone you know belongs to a club, see if you can join, too. You can also ask a librarian or local stamp dealer about clubs for kids in your area. Turn to page 38 to find out about a cross-Canada kids stamp club that you can join by mail.

Dealers

Stamp dealers can help you find the stamps you're looking for. They'll also let you know about new stamps, other collectibles and much more. Most dealers in Canada specialize in selling Canadian stamps, but some also carry stamps from other countries. To find a dealer, attend a stamp show, ask at your stamp club, or look for dealers' ads in stamp magazines, such as *Canadian Stamp News* and *The Canadian Philatelist*.

You can buy stamp magazines at news-stands or borrow them from the library.

Auctions

Attending an auction is another way to buy stamps and other postal items. Stamps sold at auctions are usually more valuable than stamps found at shows. To find out how valuable, take a look at the auction catalogue. It describes the stamps to be auctioned and how much money will probably be bid for them.

Auctions can be very exciting and rather confusing. If possible, go to your first auction with an experienced collector. Your club or stamp dealer may hold auctions or know about upcoming ones.

Stamp shows

To get stamp information or to buy stamps, catalogues, equipment and more, go to a stamp show. You'll meet stamp dealers and other collectors and get the latest information on stamps. For information about shows in your area, check the newspaper or ask your stamp dealer or other members of your club.

Before you go to a show:
• Make a list of stamps you want for your collection. Otherwise you may buy something you already own.

• Take along your tongs, magnifying glass and a stiff envelope to safely hold any stamps you buy.

• Use your magnifier to check stamps carefully before you buy them. Look for tears, stains and other damage. Faults are often more obvious on the backs of stamps.

COLLECTING CANADIAN STAMPS

Even if you don't have a stamp dealer or club in your neighbourhood, it's easy to collect Canada's stamps. Philatelic centres and many postal outlets across Canada carry the latest stamps as well as information about them.

If your nearest postal outlet doesn't carry a full selection of stamps, write to:

National Philatelic Centre
75 St. Ninian Street
Antigonish, NS B2G 2R8

You can also call, free, 1-800-565-4362.

You'll receive a catalogue of stamp-related things to buy, including books, videos, sweatshirts and posters.

Canada Post Corporation even has a stamp-collecting club especially for kids called The Stamp Travellers' Club. For $14.95, members receive a starter kit that includes stamps, tongs, magnifier, binder and more. Newsletters and other information about Canadian stamps are sent to members five times a year. These are filled with contests, tips, jokes, puzzles and quizzes. Members who order stamps through the club also receive a special bonus of mounts. To find out more, write:

The Stamp Travellers' Club
c/o Canada Post Corporation
National Philatelic Centre
75 St. Ninian Street
Antigonish, NS B2G 2R8

Or call the toll-free number:
1-800-565-CLUB.

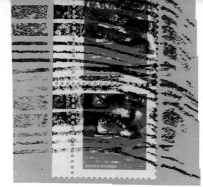

MORE STAMP TALK

Bogus: A fake stamp. It can be from a country that doesn't exist or about a made-up event and is often created by crooks to fool collectors.

Cachet: A message and or picture printed on an envelope to mark a special event.

Cancellation: A mark put on a stamp so that it can't be reused. Cancelling may be done by a cancelling machine or with a hand stamp or a pencil. A date, time and location are usually included in the cancellation. A cancellation is a type of postmark.

Cinderella: Something printed to look like a stamp, even though it's not a stamp. Cinderellas are often printed for special events, such as exhibitions, Christmas and so on.

Fake: A real stamp or postmark that's been changed. For example, a stamp with a low price on it may be changed to a more expensive one.

Fault: Any damage to a stamp, such as missing perforations, tears, stains or thinning of the paper.

Flaw: An error, usually small, that occurs when a stamp is being printed.

Gutter: The space between rows of stamps on a sheet; usually plain but sometimes printed with coloured circles. (See "traffic lights.")

Killer: A very heavy postmark on a stamp, like the one above. The postmark may cover the stamp's design completely. Also called an obliterator.

Overprint: Words or numbers printed on an already existing stamp to mark an event that occurs after the stamp is printed or to increase the stamp's value.

Postmark: Lines or markings printed on mail when it passes through the post office. It shows when and where the letter was posted. If the postmark marks, or "cancels," the stamp, it's called a cancellation.

Skip: A stamp that has been used to post a letter but has not been cancelled.

Socked on the nose: A postmark that is easy to read, circular and printed in the middle of a stamp. These postmarks are difficult to find.

Space-filler: A stamp in poor condition that fills a hole in your collection until you can afford a better stamp.

Traffic lights: The coloured circles that appear in the border of sheets of stamps. The colours of the circles are the colours used to print the stamps.

Undenominated: Stamps with no value or postage rate printed on them.

INDEX

albums, 8, 13, 16–17
artists, 6, 22, 23
auctions, 8, 37

blocks, 31
booklets, 34
borderlines, 6
British Guiana, 1856 one-cent
    stamp, 4, 33

Canada Post Corporation
    (CPC), 22–23, 38
catalogues, 7, 9, 37
Christmas, 5, 32
clubs, 8, 36–37, 38
coils, 31
colour guides, 9
commemoratives, 10
constant varieties, 24

dealers, 8, 28, 36–37
definitives, 10
denominations, 7, 23
descriptions, 6
designers, 6

E-mail, 19
errors, 24–25

face values, 7
faults, 30, 37
first-day covers, 34
Fleming, Sir Sandford, 5

guides, 9
gum, 7, 8, 30

Hill, Sir Rowland, 19
hinges, 9, 13, 16, 30

inconstant varieties, 25
inverted centres, 24

magazines, 37
magnifying glasses, 9, 37

mail, 18–19
margins, 6, 30
mint stamps, 11, 30
mounts, 9, 13

National Philatelic Centre, 38

oddities and freaks, 25

panes, 23
paper, 19, 23, 25, 30
paper folds, 25
parts, 6–7
Penny Black, 4, 19, 32
perfing errors, 25
perforation guides, 9
perforations, 6, 23, 25, 30
philatelists, 10
philately, 10
pictorials, 10
post office marks, 35
post offices, 7, 21
postal services, 18–19, 20–21
postmarks, 7, 30, 34
prepacks, 15
press sheets, 23
printers, 7, 23
printing shifts, 25
proofs, 23

Queen Elizabeth II, 32, 33

semi-postals, 11
se-tenants, 31
shows, 8, 37
souvenir sheets, 35
special issues, 11
Stamp Travellers' Club, The, 38
stamps
    biggest, 4
    Canada's first, 5
    Canadian, 5, 14–15, 17,
      21, 22–23, 24–25, 26, 38

caring for, 12–13
creating, 22–23
deciding what to collect,
    14–15, 31, 37
errors, 24–25
first, 4, 19, 32
first Christmas, 5
first diamond-shaped, 5
first "do-it-yourself," 26
first self-adhesive, 26
groups of, 31
international, 9, 28–29,
    32–33
invention of, 18–19
mint, 11, 30
obtaining, 8, 36–37, 38
odd shapes, 5, 26
parts, 6–7
rarest, 4, 33
removing from envelopes,
    12
smallest, 4
sticking in album, 8, 13,
    16–17
stories about, 32–33
terms, 6–7, 10–11, 24–25,
    30–31, 34–35, 39
types, 10–11
unusual, 4–5, 24–25,
    26–27, 32–33
used, 11, 30
strips, 31
subjects, 14–15, 16

Three-Penny Beaver, 5, 27
tongs, 8, 37
tweezers. see tongs
twins, 31

used stamps, 11, 30

weird stamps, 26–27